TO:

_____

FROM:

_____

MESSAGE:

_____

_____

_____

DATE:

_____

MY EVERYTHING GRATITUDE JOURNAL

31-Day Gratitude Journal for Self-Care and
Empowerment
with Bonus Goal Setting Guide

Sharon J. Lawrence, LCSW-C

ISBN: 9781799053606

Cover Editing by Sharon J. Lawrence

Editing by Womack Consulting Group

Author Photo Credit: ACGP Photography/ Russell Young

This journal is dedicated to my husband for loving me through every journey and to everyone who has been a part of my growth. I am eternally GRATEFUL TO GOD for you all!!

Special thank you to Alexis Booker, Sylvia Epps, Brenda Ward, and Erica Reed!! In your own special way, you have contributed your time, input, encouragement, and love in everything I do for Selah Wellness! I am grateful to call you family!!!

Introduction

My main reason for creating the My Everything 31-Day Gratitude Journal was to help others find their inner strength which will lead to self-preservation, emotional growth, and overall gratefulness. Being grateful is the power of knowing how much you have, despite what may be going on around you. Being grateful also means that others may not see your worth, but that you are able to see it.

This is not your typical journal. It will touch on Everything and every area in your life, allowing you to assess your overall gratitude and access a portal of new hope. You will do more than just write about your day, you will write from a more positive perspective. Over the next 31 days, this journal will shift your thinking about yourself, your circumstances, your relationships, and your level of gratitude.

I should warn you, that when you begin to change for the better, the outcome will be contagious. I ask that you share your gratitude stories with others to encourage them and to receive confirmation for your growth and positivity.

As you prepare for this 31-Day journey, please make a commitment to yourself to be honest about your feelings and what you hope to get out of this. This is not the time to shrink back or to minimize anything that comes your way. However, it is time to reflect and think about the good things that are about to be manifested in your life.

Enjoy the journey! May your "Everything" be changed!!!

-

CONTENTS

"For many, life is good, but it's even better when you can enjoy a good laugh. Laughter has the ability to heal your heart and mood! Laugh today!!!"
– Sharon J. Lawrence

DAY 1: LAUGHTER

QUOTE OF THE DAY:

"For many, life is good, but it's even better when you can enjoy a good laugh. Laughter has the ability to heal your heart and mood! Laugh today!!!"
– Sharon J. Lawrence

MESSAGE OF THE DAY:

Finding laughter in the simplest of things can keep you smiling all day. Laughter is not only good for the soul, but it is good for your thought process. It keeps you smiling and spreading joy to others who may need it more than you. Today, as you embark on this new journey with your Gratitude Journal, start with some joy, a good laugh, and a smile to guide you for the next thirty days. Look for the good things that bring you laughter!!! Learn to listen to your laughter and get used to hearing yourself enjoy each moment.

Entry Date: 10/8/19

Share something that you are grateful for when it comes to laughter. What makes you laugh? Is there something that causes you to spread laughter among others?

True Laughter-the kind that reaches deep, past painful emotions of the day or life - that laughter makes life worth living. I can only think of a few people who make me laugh like that - Tomeika and Rickea from college, and Shandae. I know other people make me smile and laugh, but it can tend to be surface level. Pure, unadulterated honesty makes me laugh - when someone

even in humor, vents how they really
feel-I laugh in relief and pleasure,
because I'm so often not honest about
myself-to others. Pure goofiness makes
me laugh too. I'm an adult, but I miss
playing like a kid-and the freedom that
comes with it. I do tend-to spread
laughter to others though. I meet
strangers and can drum up laughter.
Is there something though that causes
me-to spread laughter among others?
I don't want others-to be sad or hurt.
I know what that feels like. And I

want to be a person God uses to
dig up joy, encouragement,
happiness because it only takes one
kind word or gesture for someone to
keep going. When I came home from
ECSU, the kindness of others —
laughing with Adam and Jeannine —
those things saved me. Laughter can
break up the heaviness.

DAY 2: FAITH

QUOTE OF THE DAY:

"Faith requires action and movement. Once you voice that you believe in something, take one step at a time and watch provision be made."
- Sharon J. Lawrence

MESSAGE OF THE DAY:

Faith has been my guide for many years. I cannot say that it has been a part of my entire life, but I can say that in my late teens I learned the meaning of faith and the power it holds in things coming to pass. Since then, faith has been a staple in my life. When I reflect on how faith has manifested answered prayers in my life, I am confident that faith continues to be necessary on my journey of gratitude. I am grateful for faith because it keeps me positive in the most difficult situations. Let faith be a staple in your life and in your desires and dreams.

Entry Date: _____

Today, please focus on what you are grateful today?

What is the best part about your day that you believe

faith had a factor in?

_____

_____

_____

_____

_____

_____

_____

_____

_____

15

_____

_____

_____

_____

_____

_____

_____

_____

_____

_____

_____

My Everything

_____

_____

_____

_____

_____

_____

_____

_____

_____

_____

_____

DAY 3: MOVEMENT

QUOTE OF THE DAY:

"Once you replace negative thoughts with positive ones, you'll start having positive results."
– Willie Nelson

MESSAGE OF THE DAY:

Movement is about going forward and continuously working towards your goals. It is the process of being able to see your future despite any historical events that have impacted you negatively. Moving forward means that you have the right and the opportunity to write your script. You own the rights to your musical beat and the words that guide your journey. Today is the day you can identify what you are grateful for and how it helps to move you along your new path.

Entry Date: _____

Please write something that you hope to experience as you move forward in life.

_____

_____

_____

_____

_____

_____

_____

_____

_____

_____

_____

_____

_____

_____

_____

_____

_____

_____

_____

_____

My Everything

_____

_____

_____

_____

_____

_____

_____

_____

_____

_____

_____

_____

DAY 4: PRIORITIES

QUOTE OF THE DAY:

"Make sure YOU are on your list of priorities! YOU cannot be at your best if YOU are not prioritizing YOU!! Self-care is a priority!!"
– Sharon J. Lawrence

MESSAGE OF THE DAY:

We prioritize everything and everyone, but we often fail to prioritize ourselves. Today is a great day to change this behavior. We must learn that we are important and that we are powerful enough to impact nations one person at a time. If you believe this, let's start now. Let's highlight our importance and our worth by using self-affirmations to influence self-confidence. Remember, you are a priority!!!

Entry Date: _____

Identify what you have learned about priorities. What are you grateful for in regard to making yourself a priority?

_____

_____

_____

_____

_____

_____

_____

_____

_____

_____

_____

_____

_____

_____

_____

_____

_____

_____

_____

My Everything

_____

_____

_____

_____

_____

_____

_____

_____

_____

_____

_____

DAY 5: TIME

QUOTE OF THE DAY:

"Time waits for no one. Use it wisely.
Value it. Don't waste it. Appreciate it.
Make sure to enjoy each moment of it."
– Sharon J. Lawrence

MESSAGE OF THE DAY:

Time is precious because it does not wait on anyone.
Imagine if we functioned like time and moved without
thinking about other's opinions and judgments.
Imagine if you had the courage to periodically move
without permission. If time waits for no one, do you
realize how important it is to live out your dreams and
visions? Value your time and the space it provides for
you to fulfill your heart's desires. Appreciate time
and make it work for you.

Entry Date: _____

In your entry, make a small list of how time has impacted you and what you are grateful for in this moment.

_____

_____

_____

_____

_____

_____

_____

_____

_____

_____

_____

_____

_____

_____

_____

_____

_____

_____

_____

_____

My Everything

_____

_____

_____

_____

_____

_____

_____

_____

_____

_____

_____

"Time waits for no
one. use it wisely.
Value it. Don't waste
it.
Appreciate it. Make
sure to enjoy each
moment of it."
-Sharon J. Lawrence

Special Message

Congratulations, on making it through the first 5 days!

You are off to a great start and seem to be motivated to continue working. If you have noticed, I have given you a little prompt to guide your journaling. It was strictly to help with focusing. For Days 6-31, you will continue to receive a motivational quote, message, and a prompt. However, you have the choice to continue following this guide or you can choose what your gratitude journal entry looks like moving forward. Be sure to focus on gratitude in each particular area if you choose to detour from the prompts.

Enjoy!!!

- *Sharon*

DAY 6: SELF - TALK

QUOTE OF THE DAY:

"Encouraging yourself begins with how you speak to yourself. Be your own biggest fan, your biggest supporter and encourager! Tell yourself that YOU ARE AWESOME!!"
– Sharon J. Lawrence

MESSAGE OF THE DAY:

Many are afraid of speaking to themselves except when they are mumbling or complaining. If this is you, let's make a change today. Today is about implementing a self-esteem boost. It is about making sure you change the way you speak to yourself about you and your movement. If you find the time to incorporate self-affirmations into your daily routine, be sure that throughout the day you only speak positive messages to yourself. If you find a negative statement surfacing, quickly correct this by reframing (rephrasing) and verbalizing something positive. Give it a try.

Entry Date: _____

Consider your thought patterns and how you will

choose to speak differently to yourself.

_____

_____

_____

_____

_____

_____

_____

_____

_____

_____

33

My Everything

_____

_____

_____

_____

_____

_____

_____

_____

_____

_____

35

DAY 7: MOTIVATE

QUOTE OF THE DAY:

"Motivation is necessary to achieve goals. Motivate someone today. Your words may be what is needed to catapult them to the next level."
– Sharon J. Lawrence

MESSAGE OF THE DAY:

We all have the power to make an impact with our message. The impact can either be positive or negative. Motivation is about empowering others. We also need motivation and sometimes that motivation comes from within. Once you motivate yourself today, plan to spread the motivation to others. Share the wealth.

Entry Date: _____

Think of a moment when you have been motivated or
when you have motivated someone. Think of ways to
repeat a moment like this.

_____

_____

_____

_____

_____

_____

_____

_____

_____

37

My Everything

DAY 8: KEYS TO THE VISION

QUOTE OF THE DAY:

"We often hear, when one door closes, another door opens. What about when a door you were expecting to open never does? No worries. Use the keys within to open another door to greatness. It's called vision."
– Sharon J. Lawrence

MESSAGE OF THE DAY:

The quote above was inspired when I learned that I have the keys to open alternate doors when opportunities were closed to me. I learned that I could believe for anything related to greatness and purpose. Today, please be encouraged to live out your vision. Remember to journal about your heart's desires and begin creating a plan of action that you can execute. Do not let the naysayers or the closed doors dictate how you move forward. Be motivated toward greatness!!!

Entry Date: _____

What does having a vision mean to you?

_____

_____

_____

_____

_____

_____

_____

_____

_____

_____

_____

_____

_____

_____

_____

_____

_____

_____

_____

_____

_____

My Everything

_____

_____

_____

_____

_____

_____

_____

_____

_____

_____

_____

DAY 9: POSITIVITY

QUOTE OF THE DAY:

"Imagine the impact that can be made by sharing positive information more than you share negative information. Food for thought."
– Sharon J. Lawrence

MESSAGE OF THE DAY:

Depending on what you have encountered in life or even in this year, it may be difficult to remain positive. Life has the ability to hit you with a one-two punch. I am here to inform you that a positive message or action has the power to change your disposition, outlook on life, and your message. Deciding to be positive allows you to change within and to change the atmosphere around you. Being positive can be a lifestyle like becoming a vegan. You choose what goes into your body. Choose to absorb goodness so that you can exude positivity. The power of positivity is yours!!

Entry Date: _____

Think of something positive that took place over the past 24 to 48 hours.

_____

_____

_____

_____

_____

_____

_____

_____

_____

My Everything

DAY 10: RELATIONSHIP WITH SELF

QUOTE OF THE DAY:

"The relationship with yourself sets the tone for every other relationship you have."
– Author Unknown

MESSAGE OF THE DAY:

Have you thought about the relationship you have with yourself? If not, take note of how you treat yourself, how much you care about yourself and the way you talk to yourself. How you treat YOU helps others to recognize your importance and worth. In essence, you treat yourself with respect so that others learn how to treat you. Today is a great day to begin establishing a relationship with yourself. Love yourself! Respect yourself! Teach others how to treat YOU! Have a GREAT relationship with YOURSELF!!

Entry Date: _____

Describe your relationship with yourself.

_____

_____

_____

_____

_____

_____

_____

_____

_____

_____

My Everything

_____

_____

_____

_____

_____

_____

_____

_____

_____

_____

_____

51

My Everything Check-In #1!

CHECK-IN TIME:

This is where you check in with yourself and assess your gratitude.

1) List three things you are grateful for in this very moment.

2) List two things you wish you were more grateful for.

3) What is one thing you have learned about yourself over the last 10 days?

_____

_____

_____

_____

_____

_____

_____

_____

53

My Everything

_____

_____

_____

_____

_____

_____

_____

_____

_____

_____

"Nothing is
impossible; the word
itself says, "I'm
possible!"

— Audrey Hepburn

DAY 11: PURPOSE

QUOTE OF THE DAY:

"Walking in your purpose is the best thing you can do for you!!"
– Sharon J. Lawrence

MESSAGE OF THE DAY:

Walking in your purpose is something that can be extremely scary. However, one of the best lessons that you can learn about yourself is learning what you have been called to do. We all have been chosen to make an impact on the world even if that is one person at a time. Let this be the moment you decide that regardless of the fear and uncertainty, you are going to learn and understand your purpose and then you are going to walk in it with boldness.

Entry Date: _____

Do you know your purpose? How much thought have you given to your purpose?

_____

_____

_____

_____

_____

_____

_____

_____

_____

My Everything

_____

_____

_____

_____

_____

_____

_____

_____

_____

_____

_____

DAY 12: I'M POSSIBLE

QUOTE OF THE DAY:

"Nothing is impossible; the word itself says, 'I'm possible!"
– Audrey Hepburn

MESSAGE OF THE DAY:

This is one of my most favorite quotes. Often, we think that it's impossible to achieve what others consider unachievable based on their own opinions. I've learned that your dreams can be manifested by you believing in your ability to achieve anything. The moment you believe and set an action plan in place is the very moment when you realize that you are capable of doing anything, especially the impossible. Today is an amazing day to be grateful for the ability to conquer anything. Believe in yourself and what you are capable of doing. Be mindful of the words you use when you are speaking about your abilities. Now, go and set some amazing goals for yourself.

61

Entry Date: _____

Consider the things you can accomplish when you

know it is possible to achieve anything!

_____

_____

_____

_____

_____

_____

_____

_____

_____

My Everything

_____

_____

_____

_____

_____

_____

_____

_____

_____

_____

_____

_____

DAY 13: LOVE THYSELF

QUOTE OF THE DAY:

"Increasing self-love is key to appreciating who you are and who you are becoming."
–Sharon J. Lawrence

MESSAGE OF THE DAY:

Today is one of those days where I'm asking you to take a moment and evaluate how much you love yourself. It is also one of those days where I want you to be grateful for the opportunity to love yourself even more than you may already. Appreciating yourself and understanding your self-worth allows you to show others how to treat you. Loving yourself helps people to understand your importance and that you have value in this world. It shows you how awesome you are! I challenge you today to love yourself so that you can love others and teach them how to love you.

Entry Date: 10/9/19

How do you love yourself in a healthy way?

I don't think I do. A few months ago in June, a friend told me it was observable that I didn't love myself. He felt I had low self-esteem because I continued to compromise for the love of someone else. So how much do I love myself? Not much. Do I even like myself? I love others by patiently listening to them, being kind to them, meeting their needs if necessary, encouraging them, believing in their potential + growth, etc. I don't even give myself that much - patience, kindness, honesty, forgiveness, grace.

Its hard to love myself because of

my flaws / faults, so I avoid myself

altogether. As a child, and growing up,

my Dad didn't accept bad grades, bad

behavior, or even us really. I felt he didn't

like me for who I was, so I began to be

someone else. I figured- I will like horses,

farming- anything he likes, and then he'll

look at me. All the bad we can ignore. So

now, as an adult, I still ignore my "bad"-

the unlovable parts of me = my personal

feelings, my inability to speak up, when I

fail or make a mistake, if I want to do

67

something different, my need for rest/
"weakness", my proneness to depression.
But in essence, I'm repeating my dads
behavior and ignoring me now too. If he
ignored me, I am not worth paying attention
to. And so I don't. How do you love someone
you don't acknowledge or you don't know?
I tend to teach others to love me like my
dad- ignoring me, not really knowing me,
not admitting fears or faults. I'm grateful
I'm realizing this so by 30, I can start
living, thinking, loving differently. I want
to learn to love myself.

DAY 14: PROJECT MANAGEMENT

QUOTE OF THE DAY:

"You are the project manager of your own life, yes, you are!"
–Sharon J. Lawrence

MESSAGE OF THE DAY:

Have you ever met someone who always needed the opinions of others or was waiting for another person's approval before they made their next move? Are you that individual who constantly waits on someone to guide you every step of the way? It is imperative that you learn that you are the project manager of your own life. You are the one who at some point has to make decisions without the influence of others. Once you realize that you have a voice and a choice based on God's divine plan, you will realize that you are also the decision-maker for every move you make on your journey called life. Be in control today. Today is the day that you get to choose what's best for you and what your next steps will look like. Trust God and not man.

69

Entry Date: _____

Think of ways to manage your life and the areas that require more attention.

_____

_____

_____

_____

_____

_____

_____

_____

_____

_____

My Everything

_____

_____

_____

_____

_____

_____

_____

_____

_____

_____

_____

_____

_____

_____

_____

_____

_____

_____

_____

_____

_____

_____

DAY 15: UNDERSTANDING GRATEFULNESS

QUOTE OF THE DAY:

Jeremiah 29:11- "For I know the plans I have for you, 'declares the LORD, 'plans to prosper you and not harm you, plans to give you hope and a future." (NIV)

MESSAGE OF THE DAY:

Gratefulness is having the ability to be appreciative, happy, and humbled by what has been done for you. Gratefulness also brings a heavy heart that confirms the appreciation you feel. If you've never experienced gratefulness, I challenge you to think of a moment when you have been truly appreciative for something that has been done to impact your life.

73

Entry Date: _____

How can you show your gratitude towards others

over the course of the next week?

_____

_____

_____

_____

_____

_____

_____

_____

_____

My Everything

_____

_____

_____

_____

_____

_____

_____

_____

_____

_____

_____

75

DAY 16: BALANCE

QUOTE OF THE DAY:

"Focus on being balanced - success is balance."
- Laila Ali

MESSAGE OF THE DAY:

Every time I think of balance, I think of the balance beam in my middle school gymnastics class. The balance beam was one of my favorite activities. It required me to be in control of my mind and my physical being. Being balanced in life means that you are looking at multiple areas that not only require your attention but also care. In order to have true balance, it is necessary to pay attention to all areas of your life, ensuring that each receives the needed attention at the right time. It is impossible to do everything at the same time, but you can put everything into perspective so that you are living a balanced life. Make sure that you're not being pulled in so many different ways that it causes you to be off-balance.

77

Entry Date: _____

Complete the sentence:

In order to have balance, I need _____.

_____

_____

_____

_____

_____

_____

_____

_____

_____

My Everything

DAY 17: RISK TAKER

QUOTE OF THE DAY:

"Life is either a daring adventure or nothing at all."
— Helen Keller, The Open Door

MESSAGE OF THE DAY:

Don't be afraid. The risks are there so that you can step out on faith and accomplish what you have been called to do. Whether it's a new job, relationship, or a new venture, it requires risk. We don't always know what the outcome is going to be, but we will never know if we don't take the risk. I have taken many risks to get where I am today and I am sure that if I did not take them, I would still be where I was 25 years ago. If you are still afraid after reading this message, I encourage you to *do it afraid*. Take the risk!

Entry Date: _____

What do you feel when you think of taking risks to

accomplish your goals?

_____

_____

_____

_____

_____

_____

_____

_____

_____

My Everything

_____

_____

_____

_____

_____

_____

_____

_____

_____

_____

_____

DAY 18: SET APART

QUOTE OF THE DAY:

"We are not set apart to rule but chosen and set apart to serve."
- Theodore M. Burton

MESSAGE OF THE DAY:

Set apart means that you cannot roll, mingle, and hang with every single person or group that you come in contact with. Set apart means that there is something different about YOU. It doesn't mean that you're better than anyone, but it does mean that you are the best version of you and that the mandate on your life requires that you not lose focus on the mission you have been called to fulfill in life.

Entry Date: _____

What makes you different or unique from others?

_____

_____

_____

_____

_____

_____

_____

_____

_____

My Everything

_____

_____

_____

_____

_____

_____

_____

_____

_____

_____

_____

_____

_____

_____

_____

_____

_____

_____

_____

_____

_____

_____

DAY 19: FOCUSED

QUOTE OF THE DAY:

"When you focus on being a blessing, God makes sure that you are always blessed in abundance."
-Joel Osteen

MESSAGE OF THE DAY:

My husband always says that my work ethic is like none other. I laugh because sometimes I feel like I'm not focused enough. But when I talk to my husband, friends, and family they all tend to remind me of how focused and committed I am. I've learned from their messages that focus is necessary to accomplish one's goals. We do not have the luxury of being lazy when it comes to getting things done. Learn to be focused on the things that are important and related to your goals. If you find that you are focusing on minor things that have no value, it is time to shift your thinking and focus on those things that have great value and importance for your journey in life. Today is a great day to either get focused or to re-focus on

what's important to you. When you are focused, you
are successful, and others are blessed by your gifts.

Entry Date: _____

Think of ways to increase and improve your ability to focus.

_____

_____

_____

_____

_____

_____

_____

_____

_____

My Everything

_____

_____

_____

_____

_____

_____

_____

_____

_____

_____

_____

_____

93

DAY 20: EXCELLENCE

DEFINITION OF THE DAY:

Excellence:
1: the quality of being excellent.
2: an excellent or valuable quality:
virtue.
- Webster's Dictionary

QUESTION OF THE DAY:

What does excellence mean to you and how is it manifested in your life?

Entry Date: _____

How can a mindset of excellence impact your future?

_____

_____

_____

_____

_____

_____

_____

_____

_____

_____

_____

_____

_____

_____

_____

_____

_____

_____

_____

_____

_____

My Everything

My Everything Check-In #2!

CHECK-IN TIME:

This is where you check in with yourself and assess your gratitude.

1) List three things you are grateful for in this very moment.

2) List two things you wish you were more grateful for.

3) What is one thing you have learned about yourself over the last 20 days?

_____

_____

_____

_____

_____

_____

_____

_____

_____

_____

_____

_____

_____

_____

_____

_____

My Everything

_____

_____

_____

_____

_____

_____

_____

_____

_____

_____

_____

"The purpose of
our journey is to
restore ourselves
to wholeness."
- Debbie Ford

DAY 21: WHOLENESS

QUOTE OF THE DAY:

"The purpose of our journey is to restore ourselves to wholeness."
- Debbie Ford

MESSAGE OF THE DAY:

The understanding of wholeness comes from one's ability to understand that their mind, body, and spirit must be safe, secure, and fully intact. Wholeness represents one's ability to protect their total well-being. Knowing that you are whole allows you to think clearly and strategically about matters pertaining to your life, profession, family, and other relationships. Focus your mind on being whole and intact.

Entry Date: _____

What can you do to ensure that you are fostering a

mindset of wholeness?

_____

_____

_____

_____

_____

_____

_____

_____

_____

_____

_____

_____

_____

_____

_____

_____

_____

_____

_____

_____

DAY 22: FAMILY

QUOTE OF THE DAY:

"Being family is determined more by behavior than blood."
-Author Unknown

MESSAGE OF THE DAY:

The definition of family can vary from person to person. For some, family represents chaos while for others family represents a place of love and strength. Today, you have an opportunity to review your relationships and determine how you view family and its impact on your life. Whether it has been negative or positive, you have the opportunity to establish a true definition for yourself. You also have the power to redefine what family looks like to you.

Entry Date: _____
What makes you proud about family?

_____

_____

_____

_____

_____

_____

_____

_____

_____

My Everything

_____

_____

_____

_____

_____

_____

_____

_____

_____

_____

_____

_____

_____

_____

_____

_____

_____

_____

_____

_____

_____

_____

DAY 23: FRIENDSHIP

QUOTE OF THE DAY:

"Many people will walk in and out of your life, but only true friends will leave footprints, in your heart."
- Author Unknown

MESSAGE OF THE DAY:

Good friends are hard to come by. True friendships require reciprocity. Not the type that says, "if you do for me, then I'll do for you." I'm talking about the type of relationship where both individuals place a value on the relationship and are fully invested. Be grateful even if it is just one person who falls into this category. It is better than having 10 friends who may not have the ability to understand the true meaning of friendship.

Entry Date: _____

Name one person who has been a constant friend,

one who understands and supports you.

_____

_____

_____

_____

_____

_____

_____

_____

_____

My Everything

_____

_____

_____

_____

_____

_____

_____

_____

_____

_____

_____

DAY 24: I AM ENOUGH

MESSAGE OF THE DAY:

Repeat…

I AM ENOUGH!!!!!

I AM ENOUGH!!!!!

I AM ENOUGH!!!!!

I AM ENOUGH!!!!!

I AM ENOUGH!!!!!

I AM ENOUGH!!!!!

I AM ENOUGH!!!!!

Let this be your declaration today and every day!!!!

Entry Date: _____

Identify what is needed to make you feel secure in

knowing you are enough!

_____

_____

_____

_____

_____

_____

_____

_____

My Everything

_____

_____

_____

_____

_____

_____

_____

_____

_____

_____

_____

DAY 25: REJECTION

QUOTE OF THE DAY:

"We all learn lessons in life. Some stick, some don't. I have always learned more from rejection and failure than from acceptance and success."
-- Henry Rollins

MESSAGE OF THE DAY:

Rejection has its perks. Sure, that sounds really strange. We understand that rejection hurts and that it can be very disappointing. However, rejection has the ability to allow you to assess who you are and what you think about yourself. It also teaches you how to be better to yourself and how to be a friend to yourself. Rejection pushes you to believe that you are capable of doing things when no one else is there to assist or support you. The perks are that you learn to stand on your own two feet and that you realize that you are able to accomplish things without the naysayers. Today is the day that you find the good in rejection.

119

Entry Date: _____

Share how rejection can shape your thinking
positively.

_____

_____

_____

_____

_____

_____

_____

_____

_____

My Everything

DAY 26: BOUNDARIES

QUOTE OF THE DAY:

"Boundaries are necessary and beneficial to your overall emotional well-being."
- Sharon J. Lawrence

MESSAGE OF THE DAY:

Boundaries are necessary for any relationship that you have. They are like the yellow lines in the middle of the road when driving. Those yellow lines remind drivers to drive on their respective sides of the road. Just as the yellow lines have the purpose of controlling traffic, boundaries in your life dictate how people enter or interact in your life. If boundaries are not in place, you run the risk of allowing people to enter into areas of your life where they should not be or have not been officially welcomed. Learn to establish clear boundaries so that people understand who you are and how to respect you. Remember you can't rely on people to set the boundaries for you pertaining to your life. Only you can do that!

Entry Date: _____

Determine areas in your life that require increased boundaries.

_____

_____

_____

_____

_____

_____

_____

_____

_____

_____

_____

_____

_____

_____

_____

_____

_____

_____

_____

_____

DAY 27: MENTAL HEALTH

QUOTE OF THE DAY:

"There is no health without Mental Health."
- David Satcher

MESSAGE OF THE DAY:

Having good mental health means that you are mentally well and that you are giving attention to maintaining this level of health in your life. As a therapist, I can assure you that we do not have the luxury of ignoring the symptoms of mental illness or not dealing with stressors that impact our overall emotional well-being. You have an obligation to yourself to ensure that you are committed to your emotional health. It is non-negotiable. It is necessary. If you are concerned that people are going to judge you for getting help, don't be. It is important that you are OK. There is help available. I encourage you to make the call today to speak with someone who can help NOW.

127

Entry Date: _____

List 3 ways to focus on your mental health.

_____

_____

_____

_____

_____

_____

_____

_____

_____

My Everything

_____

_____

_____

_____

_____

_____

_____

_____

_____

_____

_____

_____

DAY 28: TRANSITION

QUOTE OF THE DAY:

"Your life does not get better by chance, it gets better by change."
- Jim Rohn

MESSAGE OF THE DAY:

Often when people think of transition, they think of a person passing away. When I think of transition, I think of moving from one phase of our life to another in regard to work, relationships, and our emotional mindset. I love the power of transition because it allows me to learn something new about myself and how I interact with others. Imagine understanding what transition looks like for you when you make the decision to do something new, something greater, something phenomenal. What does transition look like for you? Think of all the ways that you can make transitions in your life so that you can be who you are supposed to be!

131

Entry Date: _____

In transition, what is something you can do to make

today a better day?

_____

_____

_____

_____

_____

_____

_____

_____

My Everything

133

DAY 29: FINANCES

QUOTE OF THE DAY:

"Stay on top of your finances. Don't leave that up to others."
- Leif Garrett

MESSAGE OF THE DAY:

Thinking of finances is about setting priorities in place. Even if your finances are not where they should be, it is never too late for you to consider where you would like to see yourself financially. Do you have a financial plan? Do you have financial goals? Do you have a spreadsheet that helps you manage your funds on a monthly basis? Whatever your structure and strategy, looking at your finances should be about setting priorities for your present and future. This is another area that is non-negotiable. This is the time to not only look at your finances and your goals but to ensure that those goals include retirement, generational wealth/legacy, and end of life planning.

135

Entry Date: _____

What are two ways you can begin reaching your

financial goals?

_____

_____

_____

_____

_____

_____

_____

_____

_____

My Everything

137

DAY 30: FORGIVENESS

QUOTE OF THE DAY:

"It's one of the greatest gifts you can give yourself to forgive. Forgive everybody."
- Maya Angelou

MESSAGE OF THE DAY:

Forgiveness is one of the most challenging tasks yet, the most powerful. Forgiveness allows you to release others from your anger and your pain. Forgiveness also allows you to live in peace and without the burdens of the past. Remember, forgiveness is more about your journey than it is another person's. Release them today and walk in your new freedom. Forgive!

Entry Date: _____

Identify what you have learned and how powerful it

can be to give time and attention to everything in

your life that deserves your attention.

_____

_____

_____

_____

_____

_____

_____

_____

_____

_____

DAY 31: SELAH...

MESSAGE OF THE DAY:

Now that we have come to the end of the 31-Day journey of gratitude journaling, I want you to realize and understand the meaning behind the word Selah. Selah means to pause and meditate on what you just heard or read. It comes from the Bible and is referenced by multiple spiritual leaders and scholars worldwide. It is my desire that you learn to be in a mindset where you are able to pause and reflect on the moment that you are in before moving forward. This moment in time can be powerful and empowering. Always use it for growth and strength.

Selah.

My Everything Check-In #3!

CHECK-IN TIME:

This is where you check in with yourself and assess your gratitude.

1) List three things you are grateful for in this very moment.

2) List two things you wish you were more grateful for.

3) What is one thing you have learned about yourself over the last 31-Days?

_____

_____

_____

_____

_____

_____

145

My Everything

CONGRATULATIONS!!!

You have completed the My Everything 31-Day Gratitude Journal. Along the way, you were able to gain tremendous insight into who you are and who you are becoming. Now, it is time to discuss next steps. The work is not over. You are more focused, determined, and ready to set some goals for your future. Whether they are short or long-term goals, make sure you have some listed. LOL.

I have **TWO BONUSES** for you!!!

First, you are receiving a two-year guide to develop your long-term goals and to create monthly goals. The sections are fillable so that you can start when you are ready. It is my hope that you stay the course and set monthly goals that will allow you to grow and realize how much you have to be grateful for!!!

Second, I am providing a free self-care worksheet that can be accessed by visiting *www.myselahwellness.com.*

I am so grateful that you are taking this journey!!!! Take good care of YOU!!!

148

Goal Setting

When one becomes free in their mind, they find new strength to see things clearly. You start to see things from a different perspective causing you to dream again and to dream bigger than ever before. This goal setting section is a simple tool for you to begin documenting your short and long-term goals. An undated guide has been included for you to fill in based on when you choose to begin this part of your journey. The sky is the limit, dream big, and write out every vision. Set realistic dates and timelines to complete your goals. Every time you complete a goal, remember to celebrate with the spirit of gratitude.

"The plans of the diligent lead surely to abundance." – Proverbs 21:5

Let's Begin:

I want to be sure you understand what it means to set goals. Goal setting begins with simply identifying specific and realistic goals that you hope to accomplish over a period of time. The undated charts provided will allow you to not only set goals, but to also identify the steps to reach those goals over the time frame you select. For each month, be sure to think of the small tasks that will help you to get closer to your goals. Also, remember to document the progress you make.

Ready. Set. Go.

Long Term Goals

1) _____

2) _____

3) _____

4) _____

5) _____

6) _____

7) _____

8) _____

9) _____

10)_____

Month 1 _____

Goals

    1) _____

    2) _____

    3) _____

    4) _____

Tasks

    1) _____

    2) _____

    3) _____

    4) _____

Timeline (by this date I will complete)

    1) _____

    2) _____

    3) _____

    4) _____

Month 2 _____

Goals

    1) _____

    2) _____

    3) _____

    4) _____

Tasks

    1) _____

    2) _____

    3) _____

    4) _____

Timeline (by this date I will complete)

    1) _____

    2) _____

    3) _____

    4) _____

153

Month 3 _____

Goals

   1) _____

   2) _____

   3) _____

   4) _____

Tasks

   1) _____

   2) _____

   3) _____

   4) _____

Timeline (by this date I will complete)

   1) _____

   2) _____

   3) _____

   4) _____

Month 4 _____

Goals

    1) _____

    2) _____

    3) _____

    4) _____

Tasks

    1) _____

    2) _____

    3) _____

    4) _____

Timeline (by this date I will complete)

    1) _____

    2) _____

    3) _____

    4) _____

Month 5 _____

Goals

    1) _____

    2) _____

    3) _____

    4) _____

Tasks

    1) _____

    2) _____

    3) _____

    4) _____

Timeline (by this date I will complete)

    1) _____

    2) _____

    3) _____

    4) _____

Month 6 _____

Goals

1) _____

2) _____

3) _____

4) _____

Tasks

1) _____

2) _____

3) _____

4) _____

Timeline (by this date I will complete)

1) _____

2) _____

3) _____

4) _____

157

Month 7 _____

Goals

   1) _____

   2) _____

   3) _____

   4) _____

Tasks

   1) _____

   2) _____

   3) _____

   4) _____

Timeline (by this date I will complete)

   1) _____

   2) _____

   3) _____

   4) _____

Month 8 _____

Goals

    1) _____

    2) _____

    3) _____

    4) _____

Tasks

    1) _____

    2) _____

    3) _____

    4) _____

Timeline (by this date I will complete)

    1) _____

    2) _____

    3) _____

    4) _____

Month 9 _____

Goals

    1) _____

    2) _____

    3) _____

    4) _____

Tasks

    1) _____

    2) _____

    3) _____

    4) _____

Timeline (by this date I will complete)

    1) _____

    2) _____

    3) _____

    4) _____

Month 10 _____

Goals

1) _____

2) _____

3) _____

4) _____

Tasks

1) _____

2) _____

3) _____

4) _____

Timeline (by this date I will complete)

1) _____

2) _____

3) _____

4) _____

Month 11 _____

Goals

    1) _____

    2) _____

    3) _____

    4) _____

Tasks

    1) _____

    2) _____

    3) _____

    4) _____

Timeline (by this date I will complete)

    1) _____

    2) _____

    3) _____

    4) _____

Month 12 (Year 1) _____

Goals

1) _____

2) _____

3) _____

4) _____

Tasks

1) _____

2) _____

3) _____

4) _____

Timeline (by this date I will complete)

1) _____

2) _____

3) _____

4) _____

163

Month 13 _____

Goals

   1) _____

   2) _____

   3) _____

   4) _____

Tasks

   1) _____

   2) _____

   3) _____

   4) _____

Timeline (by this date I will complete)

   1) _____

   2) _____

   3) _____

   4) _____

Month 14 _____

Goals

    1) _____

    2) _____

    3) _____

    4) _____

Tasks

    1) _____

    2) _____

    3) _____

    4) _____

Timeline (by this date I will complete)

    1) _____

    2) _____

    3) _____

    4) _____

Month 15 _____

Goals

    1) _____

    2) _____

    3) _____

    4) _____

Tasks

    1) _____

    2) _____

    3) _____

    4) _____

Timeline (by this date I will complete)

    1) _____

    2) _____

    3) _____

    4) _____

Month 16 _____

Goals

1) _____

2) _____

3) _____

4) _____

Tasks

1) _____

2) _____

3) _____

4) _____

Timeline (by this date I will complete)

1) _____

2) _____

3) _____

4) _____

167

Month 17 _____

Goals

   1) _____

   2) _____

   3) _____

   4) _____

Tasks

   1) _____

   2) _____

   3) _____

   4) _____

Timeline (by this date I will complete)

   1) _____

   2) _____

   3) _____

   4) _____

Month 18 _____

Goals

    1) _____

    2) _____

    3) _____

    4) _____

Tasks

    1) _____

    2) _____

    3) _____

    4) _____

Timeline (by this date I will complete)

    1) _____

    2) _____

    3) _____

    4) _____

Month 19 _____

Goals

   1) _____

   2) _____

   3) _____

   4) _____

Tasks

   1) _____

   2) _____

   3) _____

   4) _____

Timeline (by this date I will complete)

   1) _____

   2) _____

   3) _____

   4) _____

Month 20 _____

Goals

    1) _____

    2) _____

    3) _____

    4) _____

Tasks

    1) _____

    2) _____

    3) _____

    4) _____

Timeline (by this date I will complete)

    1) _____

    2) _____

    3) _____

    4) _____

Month 21 _____

Goals

    1) _____

    2) _____

    3) _____

    4) _____

Tasks

    1) _____

    2) _____

    3) _____

    4) _____

Timeline (by this date I will complete)

    1) _____

    2) _____

    3) _____

    4) _____

Month 22 _____

Goals

    1) _____

    2) _____

    3) _____

    4) _____

Tasks

    1) _____

    2) _____

    3) _____

    4) _____

Timeline (by this date I will complete)

    1) _____

    2) _____

    3) _____

    4) _____

Month 23 _____

Goals

   1) _____

   2) _____

   3) _____

   4) _____

Tasks

   1) _____

   2) _____

   3) _____

   4) _____

Timeline (by this date I will complete)

   1) _____

   2) _____

   3) _____

   4) _____

Month 24 (Year 2) _____

Goals

    1) _____

    2) _____

    3) _____

    4) _____

Tasks

    1) _____

    2) _____

    3) _____

    4) _____

Timeline (by this date I will complete)

    1) _____

    2) _____

    3) _____

    4) _____

REFERENCES

Excellence. (2019). In Merriam-webster.com. Retrieved from https://www.merriam-webster.com/dictionary/excellence

Unless otherwise indicated, all scripture quotations are taken from the New International Version (NIV) Bible.

RESOURCES

For a list of resources and recommended podcasts please visit: www.myselahwellness.com/resources

ABOUT THE AUTHOR

SHARON J. LAWRENCE, LCSW-C, LCSW, ACSW, EAS-C, CAMS-II, BC-TMH

Mrs. Lawrence is an Author, National Speaker, Licensed Clinical Social Worker (LCSW-C/ LCSW) (MD/VA), Certified Anger Management Specialists-II (CAMS-II), Certified Prepare-Enrich Facilitator and Trainer, Certified Life Coach, Board Certified-TeleMental Health Provider (BC-TMH), an Approved Clinical Supervisor in Social Work (MD) and credentialed as an Employee Assistance Specialist-Clinician. She also holds a Certificate in Christian Ministries from the Evangel Bible College in Upper Marlboro, MD. She has over 15 years' experience working with children, adults, couples, and families within the following settings: mental health, substance abuse, foster care, family court, and developmental disabilities.

178

Mrs. Lawrence is the owner of Selah Wellness & Therapeutic Services, LLC, where she practices as a Therapist for Therapists, Professionals and Couples. Her passion is to improve the lives of clinicians and professionals who manage the day to day responsibility of caring for others. It has been proven that this type of care can produce secondary trauma in addition to discovering and revealing past trauma and mental health challenges.

Mrs. Lawrence is committed to helping couples strengthen and revive their relationships through counseling using the Prepare-Enrich assessment and curriculum. She provides both short and long-term counseling through the use of Cognitive Behavioral Therapy, Solution Focused Therapy, Motivational Interviewing, and Eye Movement Desensitization Reprocessing (EMDR).

Mrs. Lawrence is also a Speaker, Presenter, Trainer and Blogger for subject matter topics related to mental health education, marital enrichment, self-care, and motivating entrepreneurs. She has a YouTube Channel called the My Selah Wellness

179

focused on motivating individuals towards emotional wellness. She is the creator Desserts & Discussions: The Tour focused on speaking at organizations, business, agencies, and area churches on topics related to mental health, women's empowerment, marital enrichment, relationship building, and personal growth.

To book Sharon for speaking engagements, please visit: www.myselahwellness.com/booking or email: booking@myselahwellness.com

OTHER BOOKS BY SHARON J. LAWRENCE

7 SIMPLE WAYS TO SHAPE YOUR MARRIAGE: STRATEGIES TO FEELING LOVED AND CONNECTED

Sharon offers couples simple ways to reboot their thinking around marriage and how to improve their relationships with being intentional. Each area of this book provides information on how important it is to work together with a stronger commitment to one another.

COMING SOON!

7 SIMPLE WAYS TO SHAPE YOUR
MARRIAGE: STRATEGIES TO FEELING LOVE
AND CONNECTED

THE WORKBOOK

182

CPSIA information can be obtained
at www.ICGtesting.com
Printed in the USA
BVHW031141020419
544376BV00001B/20/P

9 781799 053606